MW01631667

The Power of Gentleness

WALNUT SPRINGS PRESS

Cover design by Tracy Anderson (tracyandersonphoto.com)
Cover illustration by 123rf.com

Illustrations on pages 10, 16, 29, and 47 by Claude Monet; see page 62 for more information. Full-page watercolor illustrations on pages 1, 6–7, 15, 20–21, 30, 39, 48–49, 52, 59, and 60 by Mandy Atkin (instasgram.com/mandy.atkin.art). All other illustrations and all small watercolor embellishments by 123rf.com.

ISBN-13: 978-1-59992-250-8

Printed in China.

I invite you to not only
love each other
more
but love each other
better.

Bonnie D. Parkin

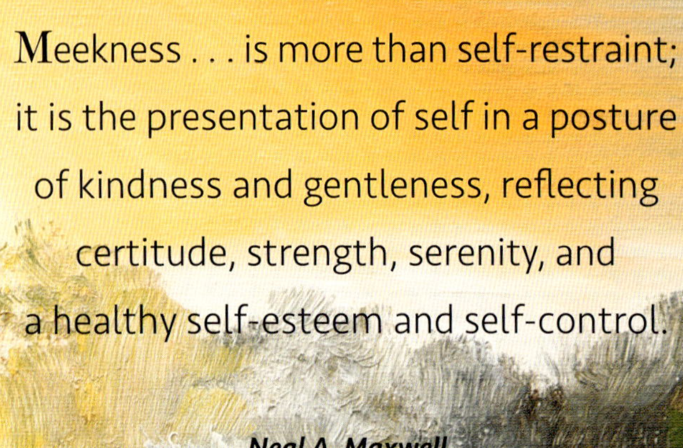

Meekness . . . is more than self-restraint; it is the presentation of self in a posture of kindness and gentleness, reflecting certitude, strength, serenity, and a healthy self-esteem and self-control.

Neal A. Maxwell

meekness

The most beautiful people have known defeat, known suffering, known struggle, known loss, and have found their way out of the depths. These persons have an appreciation, a sensitivity, and an understanding of life that fills them with COMPASSION, GENTLENESS, and a DEEP LOVING CONCERN. Beautiful people do not just happen.

Elisabeth Kubler-Ross

kindness

Kindness is the essence of greatness and the fundamental characteristic of the noblest men and women I have known. Kindness is a passport that opens doors and fashions friends. It softens hearts and molds relationships that can last lifetimes.

Kind words not only lift our spirits in the moment they are given, but they can linger with us over the years.

Joseph B. Wirthlin

Being a gentle person means that though you have the power and potential to be devastating through your attitudes and actions, you control them so that you have *a calming and soothing effect on others.*

Author Unknown

calming

charity

And charity suffereth long, and is kind,
and envieth not, and is not puffed
up, seeketh not her own, is not easily
provoked, thinketh no evil, and rejoiceth
not in iniquity but rejoiceth in the truth,
beareth all things, believeth all things,
hopeth all things, endureth all things.

Moroni 7:45

What a wonderful thing it is for you to know that your female, feminine characteristics are an endowment from God. . . . It is a holy blessing to be born with the exquisite qualities of a daughter of God. Women of God, both old and young, are spiritual and sensitive, tender and gentle. They have a kind, nurturing nature. This is your inheritance. . . . Develop the divinity that is within you. Don't dull the brightness of the spirit you came with from heaven. The Lord needs your goodness and your influence in this world.

Margaret D. Nadauld

Gentleness corrects
whatever is offensive
in our manner.

Hugh Blair

There is no end to the GOOD we can do, to the INFLUENCE we can have with others. Let us not dwell on the critical or the negative. Let us pray for STRENGTH; let us pray for capacity and desire to ASSIST OTHERS. Let us RADIATE the light of the gospel at all times and all places, that the Spirit of the REDEEMER may radiate from us.

Gordon B. Hinckley

radiate light

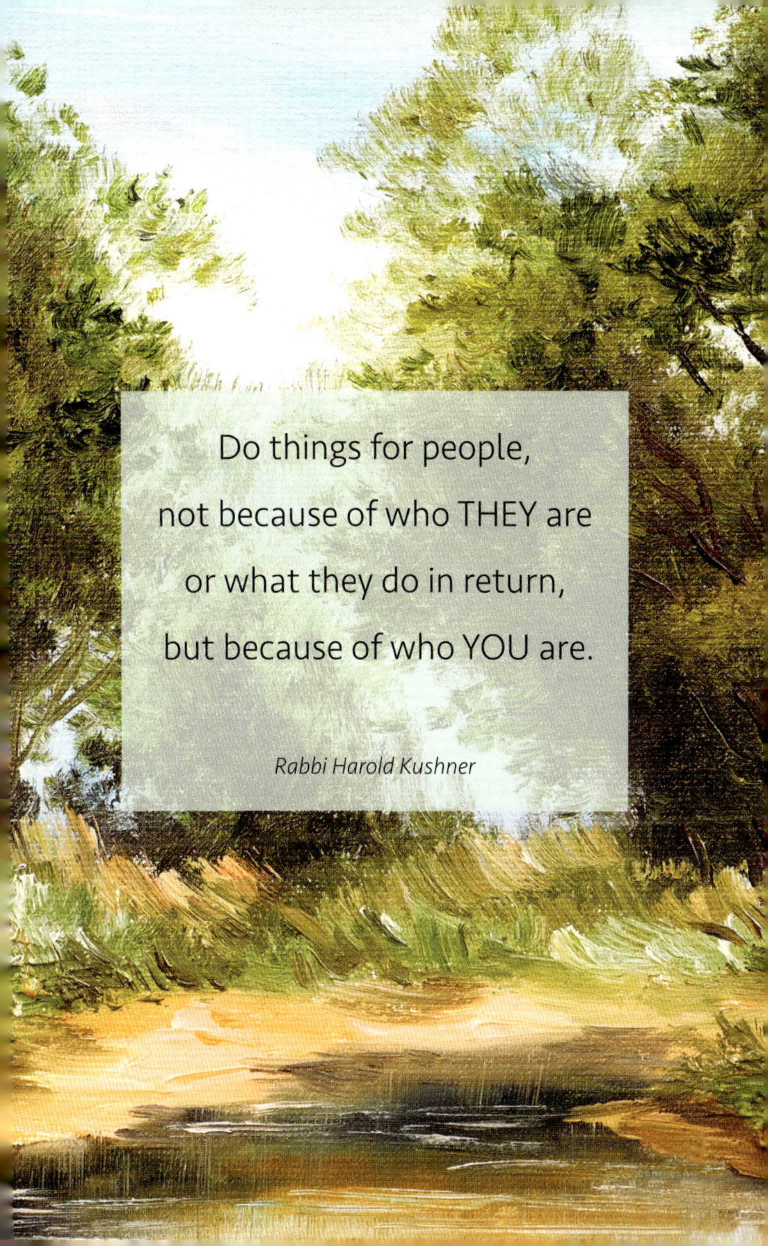
Do things for people,
not because of who THEY are
or what they do in return,
but because of who YOU are.
Rabbi Harold Kushner

But the wisdom that is from above is first pure, then peaceable, gentle, and easy to be entreated, full of mercy and good fruits, without partiality, and without hypocrisy.

James 3:17

It is indeed remarkable that the nature of our dealings with our fellowmen will determine, in large measure, our status in the kingdom of heaven. . . . We may attend to rites and rituals and yet overlook the weightier matters such as . . . kindness, honesty, mercy, virtue, and integrity. Let us never forget that if we omit them from our lives we may be found unworthy to come into [God's] presence.

Mark E. Petersen

weightier matters

humility

A Christian reveals true humility by showing the gentleness of Christ, by being always ready to help others, by speaking kind words and performing unselfish acts, which elevate and ennoble the most sacred message that has come to our world.

Ellen G. White

We believe in being honest, true,
chaste, benevolent, virtuous,
and in doing good to all men.
Article of Faith 13

I choose
GENTLENESS.
Nothing is won by force.
I choose to be gentle.

Max Lucado

Never suppress
a generous thought.

Camilla Kimball

But the fruit of the Spirit is
love, joy, peace, longsuffering,
GENTLENESS,
goodness, faith,
meekness, temperance.

Galatians 5:22-23

GENTLENESS

can only be expected

from the STRONG.

Leo Buscaglia

Let your *gentleness*

be evident to all.

Author Unknown

Kindness is the essence of a celestial life. Kindness is how a Christlike person treats others. Kindness should permeate all of our words and actions at work, at school, at church, and especially in our homes.

Joseph B. Wirthlin

There is nothing
stronger
in the world than
gentleness.
Han Suyin

I've learned that people will forget what you said, people will forget what you did, but people will never forget HOW YOU MADE THEM FEEL.

Maya Angelou

No man or woman of the humblest sort can really be strong, gentle, pure, and good, without the world being the better for it, without somebody being helped and comforted by the very existence of that goodness.

Phillips Brooks

Our greatest strength lies in the

gentleness

and tenderness of our heart.

Rumi

Femininity . . . finds expression in your qualities of your capacity to love, your spirituality, delicacy, radiance, sensitivity, creativity, charm, graciousness, gentleness, dignity, and quiet strength.

James E. Faust

spirituality

pure love of Christ

But charity is the pure love of Christ, and it endureth forever; and whoso is found possessed of it at the last day, it shall be well with him.

Wherefore . . . pray unto the Father with all the energy of heart, that ye may be filled with this love, which he hath bestowed upon all who are true followers of his Son, Jesus Christ; that ye may become the [daughters] of God; that when he shall appear we shall be like him, for we shall see him as he is; that we may have this hope; that we may be purified even as he is pure.

Moroni 7:46-48

Constant kindness

can accomplish much.

As the sun makes ice melt,

kindness causes misunderstanding,

mistrust, and hostility

to evaporate.

Albert Schweitzer

Kindness makes you the most
beautiful
person in the world,
no matter what
you look like.
Author Unknown

Love one another
as Jesus loves you.
Try to show kindness
in all that you do.
Be gentle and loving
in deed and in thought,
For these are the things
Jesus taught.

From song "I'm Trying to Be Like Jesus"

For the mountains shall depart,
and the hills be removed;
but my kindness shall not
depart from thee,
neither shall the covenant
of my peace be removed,
saith the Lord that
hath mercy on thee.

Isaiah 54:10

Not only did our Savior love all; He served all. Expand your goodness to many. Old and young can be greatly blessed by your kind service. . . . I know that we can make the world a better place, because "we believe in being . . . benevolent" (Article of Faith 13).

Mary N. Cook

True gentleness
is founded
on a sense
of what we owe to
Him who made us.

Hugh Blair

The nearer we get to our Heavenly Father, the more we are disposed to look with compassion on perishing souls; we feel that we want to take them upon our shoulders, and cast their sins behind our backs. . . . If you would have God have mercy on you, have mercy on one another.

Joseph Smith

mercy and tenderness

Courage is by no means incompatible with tenderness. On the contrary, gentleness and tenderness have been found to characterize the [people] who have done the most courageous deeds.

Samuel Smiles

So much in life depends
on our attitude. The way
we choose to see things
and respond to others
makes all the difference.
Thomas S. Monson

There is a generosity in giving,
but gentleness in receiving.
Freya Stark

Where anger is a bursting flame,
gentleness is a gentle rain.

John A. Hardon

Three things in human life are important.
The first is to be kind.
The second is to be kind.
And the third is to be kind.

Henry James

Having compassion on those who are hurting for whatever reason and then translating the response of the heart into the needed act is truly ministering as God would have us do. . . . We must recognize that life is a precious gift . . . that trust and tenderness are fragile, that we must love and serve one another, must encourage one another, forgive one another—all this not once, but over and over again. Then perhaps we shall be remembered among those on the right hand of the Lord when he shall come in his glory.

Joy F. Evans

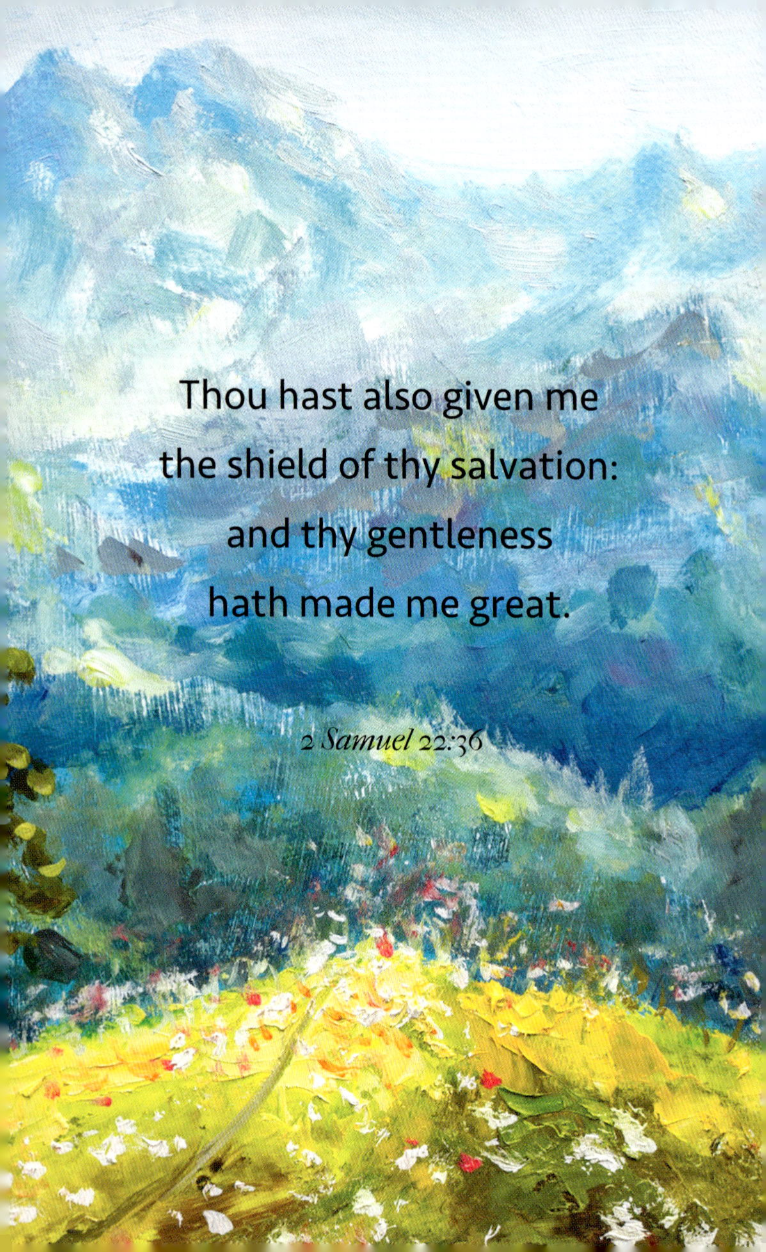
Thou hast also given me
the shield of thy salvation:
and thy gentleness
hath made me great.
2 Samuel 22:36

Kindness pardons
others' weaknesses and faults.
Kindness is extended to all—
to the aged
and the young,
to animals,
to those low of station
as well as the high.

Ezra Taft Benson

And now I would that ye should be humble, and be submissive and gentle; easy to be entreated; full of patience and long-suffering; being temperate in all things; being diligent in keeping the commandments of God at all times; asking for whatsoever things ye stand in need, both spiritual and temporal; always returning thanks unto God for whatsoever things ye do receive.

Alma 7:23

patience

When you encounter
difficulties
and contradictions,
do not try to break them,
but bend them
with gentleness and time.

St. Francis de Sales

Be gentle with people today. You don't know someone's inside struggles. Instead of being the last straw, you can be their first sign of hope.

Author Unknown

One way you can measure your value in the kingdom of God is to ask, "How well am I doing in helping others reach their potential?"

Joseph B. Wirthlin

We never know how far the effects of our service will reach. We can never afford to be cruel or indifferent or ungenerous, because we are all connected, even if it is in a pattern that only God sees.

Chieko Okazaki

How can we give to the Lord? What shall we give to him? Every kind word to our own, every help given them, is as a gift to God, whose chief concern is the welfare of his children. Every gentle deed to our neighbor, every kindness to the poor and suffering, is a gift to the Lord, before whom all mankind are equal.

every gentle

Every conformity to the Lord's plan of salvation—and this is of first importance—is a direct gift to God, for thereby we fit ourselves more nearly for our divinely planned destiny.

John A. Widtsoe

deed

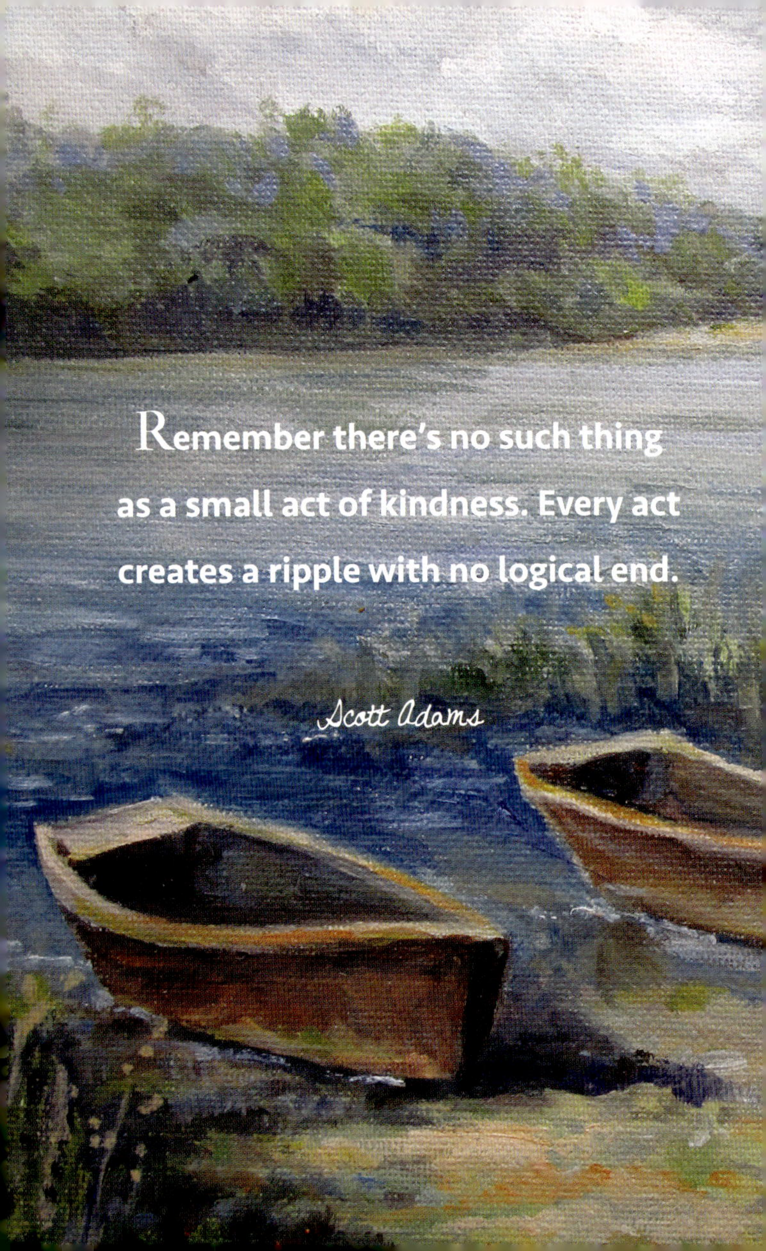
Remember there's no such thing as a small act of kindness. Every act creates a ripple with no logical end.
Scott Adams

Kindness has many synonyms—
love, service, charity.
Betty Jo N. Jepsen

The gospel provides the only way the world will ever know peace. We need to be kinder with one another, more gentle and forgiving. We need to be slower to anger and more prompt to help. We need to extend the hand of friendship and resist the hand of retribution. In short, we need to love one another with the pure love of Christ, with genuine charity and compassion and, if necessary, shared suffering, for that is the way God loves us.

Howard W. Hunter

Gratitude is the inward feeling
of kindness received.
Thankfulness is the natural impulse
to express that feeling.
Thanksgiving is the following of that impulse.

Henry Van Dyke

Let us examine our lives
and determine to follow
the Savior's example by being

KIND, LOVING,

and

CHARITABLE.

Thomas S. Monson

opportunity
Wherever there is a human being, there is an opportunity for a kindness.
Lucius Annaeus Seneca

Love and kindness
are never wasted.
They always make a difference.
They bless the one
who receives them,
and they bless you, the giver.
Barbara De Angelis
blessings

No matter what circumstances you sisters experience, your influence can be marvelously far-reaching. I believe some of you have a tendency to underestimate your profound capacity for blessing the lives of others. More often than not, it is not on the stage with some public pronouncement but in your example of righteousness and the countless gentle acts of love and kindness done so willingly, so often on a one-to-one basis.

James E. Faust

Jesus never mistreated anyone just because they mistreated Him. He confronted them in *a spirit of gentleness* and then continued *to love them.*

JOYCE MEYER

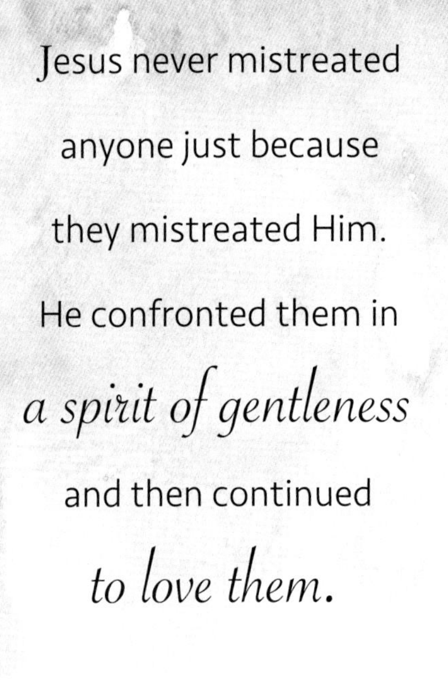

Thank you for your benevolent lives; for including those who may be different; for your kindness to your peers, the elderly, your family, and little children; for being neighbors to those who are lonely and those who have challenges and heartache. Through your benevolence, you are "pointing others to [the Savior's] light." Thank you for remembering "kindness begins with me."

Mary N. Cook

QUOTE SOURCES

Adams, Scott. https://www.brainyquote.com/quotes/scott_adams_387182.

Angelou, Maya. https://www.brainyquote.com/quotes/maya angelou_392897.

Benson, Ezra Taft. "Godly Characteristics of the Master," Oct. 1986 General Conference.

Blair, Hugh. https://awakenthegreatness within.com/35-inspirational-quotes-on-gentleness/.

Buscaglia, Leo. https://www.brainyquote.com/quotes/leo_buscaglia_131976.

Cook, Mary N. Quote on p. 33: "Remember This: Kindness Begins with Me," Apr. 2011 General Conference. Quote on p. 60: Ibid.

De Angelis, Barbara. https://www.ftd.com/blog/celebrate/kindness-quotes.

de Sales, Saint Francis. https://www.brainyquote.com/quotes/saint_francis_de_sales_143989?src=t_gentleness.

Earhart, Amelia. https://www.ftd.com/blog/celebrate/kindness-quotes.

Evans, Joy F. "'Lord, When Saw We Thee an Hungred?'" Apr. 1989 General Conference.

Faust, James E. Quote on p. 27: "Womanhood: The Highest Place of Honor," Apr. 2000 General Conference. Quote on p. 58: "You Are All Heaven Sent," Oct. 2002 General Conference.

Hinckley, Gordon B. "The Need for Greater Kindness," Apr. 2006 General Conference.

Hunter, Howard W. Satellite Broadcast Commemorating 150th Anniversary of Martyrdom of Joseph Smith. Carthage, Illinois, 26 June 1994.

"I'm Trying to Be Like Jesus" (1980). Words and Music by Janice Kapp Perry. *Children's Songbook,* no. 78. Salt Lake City: The Church of Jesus Christ of Latter-day Saints, 1989.

James, Henry. https://www.brainyquote.com/quotes/henry_james_157155.

Jepsen, Betty Jo N. "Kindness—A Part of God's Plan," Oct. 1990 General Conference.

Kimball, Camilla. As quoted by Julie B. Beck in "Relief Society: A Sacred Work," Oct. 2009 General Relief Society Meeting.

Kubler-Ross, Elizabeth. https://awakenthegreatnesswithin.com/35-inspirational-quotes-on-gentleness/.

Kushner, Harold. https://www.ftd.com/blog/celebrate/kindness-quotes.

Lucado, Max. https://awakenthegreatnesswithin.com/35-inspirational-quotes-on-gentleness/.

Maxwell, Neal A. "Meekness: A Dimension of True Discipleship," *Ensign,* Mar. 1983.

Meyer, Joyce. https://www.brainyquote.com/quotes/joyce_meyer_567569?src=t_gentleness.

Monson, Thomas S. Quote on p. 36: "First Presidency Message: Living the Abundant Life, *Liahona,* Jan. 2012. Quote on p. 55: "Kindness, Charity, and Love," Apr. 2017 General Conference.

Nadauld, Margaret D. "Hold High the Torch," Apr. 2002 General Conference.

Okasaki, Chieko. "Cat's Cradle of Kindness," Apr. 1993 General Conference.

Parkin, Bonnie D. "Choosing Charity: That Good Part," Oct. 2003 General Conference.

Petersen, Mark E. "Do Unto Others," Apr. 1977 General Conference.

Rumi. https://awakenthegreatnesswithin.com/35-inspirational-quotes-on-gentleness/.

Seneca, Lucius Annaeus. https://www.ftd.com/blog/celebrate/kindness-quotes.

Smiles, Samuel. https://awakenthegreatnesswithin.com/35-inspirational-quotes-on-gentleness/.

Smith, Joseph. *Teachings of the Prophet Joseph Smith*, comp. Joseph Fielding Smith (Salt Lake City: Deseret Book Co., 1938), 241.

Suyin, Han. https://awakenthegreatnesswithin.com/35-inspirational-quotes-on-gentleness/.

Schweitzer, Albert. https://www.ftd.com/blog/celebrate/kindness-quotes.

Stark, Freya. https://awakenthegreatnesswithin.com/35-inspirational-quotes-on-gentleness/.

Van Dyke, Henry. https://www.ftd.com/blog/celebrate/kindness-quotes.

White, Ellen G. https://www.brainyquote.com/quotes/ellen_g_white_533089?src=t_gentleness.

Widtsoe, John A. "The Gifts of Christmas," ***Ensign,*** Dec. 1972.

Wirthlin, Joseph B. Quote on p. 4: "The Virtue of Kindness," Apr. 2005 General Conference. Quotes on pp. 22 and 45: Ibid.

SELECT ILLUSTRATION CREDITS

Page 10: *Jerusalem Artichoke Flowers* (1880), by Claude Monet. https://commons.wikimedia.org/wiki/Claude_Monet_Paintings_in_Public_Domain#/media/File:Jerusalem_Artichoke_Flowers_E10330.jpg.

Page 16: *Still Life with FLowers and Fruit* (1869), by Claude Monet. https://commons.wikimedia.org/wiki/File:Still_Life_with_Flowers_and_Fruit_by_Claude_Monet,_1869,_Getty_Center.JPG.

Page 29: *Poppy Field in a Hollow Near Giverny* (1885), by Claude Monet. https://commons.wikimedia.org/wiki/Claude_Monet_Paintings_in_Public_Domain.

Page 47: *View of Vétheuil* (1880), by Claude Monet. https://commons.wikimedia.org/wiki/Claude_Monet_Paintings_in_Public_Domain#/media/File:Claude_Monet_-_View_of_Vétheuil_-_Google_Art_.